Life In Christ Workbook

By

Michelle Fortune

Life In Christ Workbook

Copyright © 2020 by Michelle Fortune

All rights reserved. No part of this book may be reproduced or transmitted in any form or by any means without written permission from the author.

ISBN (978-0-578-82787-2)

Printed in USA by Kindle Direct Publishing

CONTENTS

Dedication 1

Acknowledgments 2

Introduction 3

Life in Christ 4

Chapter One: Meditating Upon Gods Word Day And Night 5

Chapter Two: Living In Obedience According To Gods Word 17

Chapter Three: Overcoming Hindrances 28

Chapter Four: Faith In The Word 39

Chapter Five: Prayer 50

Chapter Six: Victoriously Living 64

Chapter Seven: Fellowship With One Another. 84

Chapter Eight: Renewing the Mind. 93

Chapter Nine: Witnessing. 102

Chapter Ten: Christian Leadership 113

Chapter Eleven: Live For Jesus 123

Bibliography 133

Appendix 134

About the Author 137

Dedication

This book is dedicated to my Lord and Savior Jesus Christ, and to those who desire to have a deeper relationship with our Heavenly Father.

He has given me the inspiration and desire to teach and mentor others, to grow stronger in their faith, through prayer, fasting, and studying His Word.

2 Timothy 2:15," Study to show thyself approved unto God, a workman who needeth not be ashamed, rightly dividing the word of truth."

Acknowledgments

I give all honor, glory, and praise to God who has given me the inspiration to teach, mentor, and to impact lives. I praise God for the completion of this book, and to the many lives that will be empowered in Jesus Name.

I would like to thank my entire family: To my mother Gloria Moxley & father Jerry Moxley, along with all my sisters, and brothers. I would like to especially acknowledge my sister Carmen Ikem, who has always been there to support me, and give me words of encouragement. Your discernment, knowledge, and wisdom has always guided me, and kept me on the right path. Thank you so much for being a shining light directing my path. I love you!

To my angel and best friend Adolphus Peters. You have always been there for me supporting me, praying and fasting with me. You never once hesitated when I asked you to join me in prayers. You have always encouraged me and given me words of wisdom. You have always spoken the truth, even when you knew it would hurt me. You shared my pain, and hurt when I hurt. You've always had my best interest. Words cannot express my heart felt gratitude for everything you have done for me. Thank you so much! I love you!

To Dr's. Christopher & Pamela Hardy with Lions International Training Institute. Thank you for giving me the opportunity to serve with the institute as an instructor. This has opened the door for me to impact the nations and walk in my purpose and destiny. Thank you always for your love and support and being there for me. I love you both!

Introduction

God wants us to have continual spiritual growth. He desires for us to mature not only in Christ Jesus, but also in our character, knowledge, and wisdom. He wants us to get to a place where we can stand firm in the knowledge of who He is. We can only accomplish this by studying his Word and seeking Him continually. 2 Timothy 2:15, " Study to show thyself approved unto God, a workman that needeth not be ashamed, rightly dividing the word of truth." We are saved and sanctified by grace. Through our obedience, we would see God's gracious hand guiding us and helping us to follow him. In this, we should give God thanks.

Life in Christ is about following the footsteps of Jesus. Living a life that would reflect Jesus love and character. It's about carrying the fruits of the spirit, where it will shine forth in this dark world. Let your light shine unto others, that it will cast out the darkness and bring them to a place of repentance and forgiveness. Jesus was a Glory carrier. His Glory spread throughout all the earth baptizing in the name of the Father, Son and Holy spirit. Matthew 28:19-20, "Go therefore and make disciples of all nations, immersing them in the name of the Father, and of the Son, and of the Holy Spirit, teaching them to observe all things I have commanded you. And remember, I am with you always, even to the end of the age, Amen."

Life in Christ

This book is designed to put you on the path for spiritual growth. As Christians and children of God, we are to become beacons of light, and inspiration for all the world to see, and bear witness to. We are to be wise in our decision making and counsel. We are to strive to act in a manner similar to that of Jesus Christ, with respect to how we treat one another.

You will learn how to pray, as prayer gives us strength, and brings us closer to God. You will learn how to make wise decisions that will enrich you and the lives of your family. You will study the actions of Jesus Christ and use his actions as a guide for daily life. This book will strengthen you in your found faith. The teachings will guide you through everyday life, as you walk according to God's plan and purpose, fulfilling His Kingdom here on earth.

— Michelle Fortune

CHAPTER ONE

Meditating Upon Gods Word Day and Night

Psalm 1:2-3, "But they delight in the law of the Lord, meditating on it day and night. They are like trees planted along the riverbank, bearing fruit each season. Their leaves never wither, and they prosper in all they do."

The Word of God is the foundation for a successful Christian life. We are commanded to meditate in it day and night. We should desire (ex). love to know the Word of God so that we might know more of God and grow to maturity.

The Word of God is the food of the spirit. The more we meditate on it after we study, the more our inner man is built up and renewed. You can learn how to follow God by meditating on his Word. This means, spending time reading and thinking about what you have read. It means, asking yourself how you should change, so that you will live as God wants. Knowing and thinking about God's Word, are the first steps toward applying it to your everyday life. If you want to follow God more closely, you must know what he says.

In Psalm 1:2, the "law" means all of the scripture: the first five books of Moses, the Prophets, and the other writings. The more we know of the whole scope of God's Word, the more resources we will have to guide us in our daily decisions. The more we delight in obeying God, the more fruitful we are. On the other hand, the more we allow those who ridicule God to affect our thoughts and attitudes, the more we separate ourselves from our source of nourishment, we must have contact with unbelievers if we are to witness to them, but we must not join in or imitate their sinful behavior. If we want Gods blessings, we must make friends with those who love God and his Word. When we apply God's wisdom , the fruit (results or by-products) we bear will be good and will receive God's approval. Just as a tree soaks up water and bears luscious fruit, we also are to soak up God's Word, producing actions and attitudes that honor God. To achieve anything worthwhile, we must have God's Word in our hearts.

"This book of the Law shall not depart from your mouth, but you shall meditate in it day and night, that you may observe to do according to all that is written in it. For then you will make your way prosperous, and then you will have good success."

Joshua 1:8

How to meditate on God's word is specially designed to help you develop your faith as you experience your sacred time with God and enjoying His presence.

*The **word "meditation"** in Hebrew means basically to speak or to mutter. When this is done in the heart it is called musing or **meditation**. So **meditating** on the **Word of God day and night** means to speak to yourself the **Word of God day and night** and to speak to yourself about it.*

A 7-Step Meditation Process Which Results in Revelation

1. **Write**: I copy the verse by hand onto a piece of paper or 3X5 card (Deut. 17:18) and keep it with me to meditate on, memorize and mutter throughout the

day(s). I also record this verse in my meditation/journal (which can be written, typed or verbally recorded).

2. **Quiet Down**: I become still in God's presence, loving Him through <u>soft soaking music</u> (2 Kings 3:15-16) and/or praying in tongues (1 Cor. 14:15), putting a smile on my face and picturing Jesus with me (Acts 2:25). I tune to His **flowing** thoughts, pictures and emotions (Jn. 7:37-39).

3. **Reason**: I reason together with God (Isa. 1:18), meaning the Spirit guides my reasoning process (i.e. through flow). "Lord, what do You want to show me about any of the following: the context of a verse, the Hebrew/Greek definitions of the key words in the verse, or any cultural understandings?"

4. **Speak & Imagine**: I ponder the Scripture, speaking it to myself softy over and over again until I can say it with my eyes closed. As I repeat the Scripture, I allow myself to see it with the eyes of my heart. I note what the picture is in my mind's eye as I repeat the Scripture.

5. **Feel God's Heart**: While seeing the above picture, I ask, "Lord, what does this Scripture reveal about Your heart toward me?" I feel His heart and journal it out.

6. **Hear God's *Rhema***: I put myself in the picture of this Scripture in my mind. I ask, "Lord, what are You speaking to me through this Scripture?" I tune to flowing thoughts flowing pictures (God's voice and vision) and I record this dialogue in my two-way journaling.

7. **Act**: I accept this revelation, repenting of any sin that is opposite of it, and roaring at any obstacle that stands in the way of implementing it. I then speak it forth and act on it.

Our hearts burn within as He walks with us opening Scriptures to us (Lk. 24:32).

We are transformed as we look, and see what Jesus is doing (2 Cor. 3:18).

The Holy Spirit guides the above process, leading to more or less emphasis on any of the various steps, according to God's desire for the present moment and the personal needs we have. So we remain dependent upon Him throughout.

Checklist for Tuning in to God

I Am Living the Tabernacle Experience (Heb. 8:5)

- ❖ Altar—I have laid down my own initiative, self-effort and strength.
- ❖ Laver—I cleanse myself regularly by meditating upon the Bible.
- ❖ Shewbread—My will is ground fine before God and I walk in fellowship with the Body of Christ.
- ❖ Lampstand—I have moved from my reasoning to Spirit-led reasoning.
- ❖ Incense—I am a continuous worshiper; in everything I give thanks.
- ❖ Ark—I wait before God in stillness to receive what He has for me.

I Am Applying the Tuning Dial of Habakkuk 2:1-3

- ❖ I am quieting myself down.
- ❖ I am fixing my spiritual eyes on Jesus.
- ❖ I am tuned to flow.
- ❖ I am writing down the flow of thoughts and pictures that come to me.

I Am Applying the Fine-Tuning Dial of Hebrews 10:19-22

- ❖ My heart is true, honest and sincere.
- ❖ I have absolute faith that God's river is flowing within me.
- ❖ My conscience is completely clear through Christ's cleansing blood.
- ❖ I have been obedient to God's previous *rhema*.

Testing

- ❖ I am confirming my journaling through other ways God speaks.
- ❖ My journaling lines up with Scripture and the character of God.
- ❖ My spiritual advisors confirm my journaling is from God.

Meditating Upon Gods Word Day And Night

1. Meditation is _____ the Word in our hearts, _____ it to our own souls, and personally _____ it to our own lives and circumstances.

2. Meditation begins with _____, bringing back into our minds the _____ and _____ and _____ of God.

1. Do not be conformed to this world, but be transformed by the renewal of your mind, that by testing you may discern what is the will of God, what is good and acceptable and perfect (Romans 2:2)

2. In Psalms 77, Asaph uses three verbs that capture the essence of meditation. When he finds himself perplexed and troubled and cries out to God, he determines to steady his soul by looking to God and laying hold of truth. He says in verses 11 and 12:

I will remember the deeds of the LORD;

Yes, I will remember your wonders of old.

I will ponder all your work,

And meditate on your mighty deeds (Psalms 77:11-12).

3. Asaph uses 3 verbs in the Hebrew to describe what it means to lay hold of truth: He says: I will _____, I will _____ and I will _____.

4. He begins with remembering (Zakar)—calling to mind "the deeds of the Lord" and His "wonders of old." He intentionally takes note of _____ and _____ it back into his thinking.

5. Asaph reflects on what God has accomplished for His people in the past—events and epics like the Exodus and Passover, the giving of the law on Mount Sinai, the conquest of the Promised Land. He makes an effort not to forget all the Lord has done.

6. When we_____, we think about God's Word. We dwell on it and then as opportunities arise, we preach it to ourselves.

7. We inject it into our _____ as we make decisions, as we admonish and instruct our souls to choose right things and walk down right paths.

8. This is the essence of meditation. It is _____ the truth, _____ it and _____ it in our lives. It is intentionally focusing on recalling God's truth that it might resound in our hearts and become that grid through which we sift and measure our thoughts and actions.

Fill In the blanks

- Pondering
- Psalm 77
- Remembering
- Truths
- Promises
- Embedding
- Evoking
- Meditate
- Thoughts

- Draws
- Truth
- Remember
- Praises
- Applying
- Preaching
- Remember
- Zakar
- Embracing

I. THE BIBLE

a. The bible is a book containing 66 smaller books

b. It has 2 parts- The Old Testament (OT) and the New Testament (NT)

c. The writers of the bible books are drawn from all works of life- Farmers, fisherman, statesmen, military leaders, kings/secretaries.

II. COMPARISON OF THE OLD AND NEW TESTAMENT

a. The Old Testament is about God's covenant with Israel, their shortcomings and restoration, etc.

b. The New Testament is about a new covenant made with the blood of Jesus Christ/ the son of God and God's redemption plan for mankind.

c. In the Old Testament (OT) forgiveness of sin is by shedding blood of animals' yearly, while in the New Testament (NT) forgiveness is by the shed blood of Jesus once and for all. Heb. 9:7-12.

d. Justification is by works of righteousness in the OT while justification is by faith in the NT Rom. 4:4-5.

WHY STUDY THE BIBLE

a. It is the only source of complete revelation of God and His plan for man (Jn. 5:39).

b. The Word of God has the power to discipline us and grow us up in the faith (2 Tim. 3:16-17).

c. The Word is our weapon in spiritual warfare (Ephesians 6:17).

d. The Word reveals to us our inheritance as believers (Acts 20:32).

e. It gives us encouragement and hope (Romans 15:4).

f. It gives us confidence to share the gospel (1 Peter 3:15).

III. WAYS OF KNOWING THE WORD

(a) Hearing- Romans 10:17

(b) Reading- 1 Timothy 4:14

(c) Studying- Acts 17:11

(d) Meditating- Joshua 1:8

(e) Memorizing- Psalm 119:1

(f) Applying- Hebrews 5:14

IV TOOLS FOR STUDY

a. More than one translation of the Bible (e.g). NIV, KJV, Amplified, ESV, Tyndale, NLT, ASV, Living, Good News, NAB, Scofield, The Message etc.

b. A Bible Concordance

c. A Cross-Reference Bible or Chain Reference

d. A notebook and pen

V. METHOD OF STUDY

Follow a personal Bible Study plan and make use of personal notebook to monitor 1 year plan.

VI STUDYING TO GET RESULTS

a. Approach the Bible with reverence (Proverbs 13:13).

b. Have a strong desire for wisdom (Proverbs 4:7).

c. Obey and practice the Word (James 1:21-25).

Give the Word first place in your life and you will succeed!

Notes

Notes

Notes

CHAPTER TWO

Living In Obedience According To Gods Word

Psalm 119, "Blessed are those whose is blameless, who walk in the law of the Lord."

Obedience means compliance with an order, request, or law or submission to another's authority.

For us to successfully work with God after salvation while going through life, we must continually live a life of obedience, because we walk in obedience according to the Word of God.

"We will eat the good of the land". (Isaiah 1:19).

"These are the commandments, decrees and laws the Lord your God directed to me to teach you to observe in the land that you are crossing the Jordan to possess, so that you, your children and their children after them may fear the Lord your God as long as you live by keeping all his decrees and commands that I give you, and so that you may enjoy long life. Hear, Israel, and be careful to obey so that it may go well with you and that you may increase greatly in a land flowing with milk and honey, just as the Lord, the God of your ancestor's promised you." (Deuteronomy 6:1-3).

Adam (Genesis 3) Adam lived in a perfect world and had a perfect relationship with God. His needs; he had everything. But he fell to Satan's deception.

Noah (Genesis 9) Noah and his family had survived in the flood, and the whole world was theirs. They were prosperous and life was easy. Noah shamed himself by becoming drunk, and then cursed Caanan, the son of Ham.

David (2 Samuel) David ruled well, and Israel was a dominant nation politically, economically, and military. In the midst of prosperity and success, he committed adultery with Bathsheba and had her husband Uriah murdered.

Solomon (1 Kings 11) Solomon truly had it all: power, wealth, fame, and wisdom. But his very abundance was the source of his downfall. He loved his pagan, idolatrous wives so much that he allowed himself and Israel to copy their detestable religious rites.

EIGHT REASONS WHY OBEDIENCE TO GOD IS IMPORTANT

1. Jesus Calls Us To Obedience

In Jesus Christ we find the perfect model of obedience. As his disciple, we follow Christ's example as well as his commandments. Our motivation for obedience is love:

If you love me, you will keep my commandments. (John 14:15).

2. Obedience Is An Act Of Worship

While the Bible places strong emphasis on obedience, it's critical to remember that believers are not justified (made righteous) by our obedience. Salvation is a free gift from God, and we can do nothing to merit it. True Christian obedience flows from a heart of gratitude for the grace we have received from the Lord:

"And so, dear brothers and sisters, I plead with you to give your bodies to God because of all he has done for you. Let them be a living and holy sacrifice- the kind he will find acceptable. This is truly the way to worship him." (Romans 12:1).

3. GOD REWARDS OBEDIENCE

Over and over again we read in the Bible that God blesses and rewards obedience:

"And through your descendants all the nations of the earth will be blessed-all because you have obeyed me." (Genesis 22:18).

Now if you obey me and keep my covenant, you will be my own special treasure from among all the peoples on earth; for all the earth belongs to me. (Exodus 19:5).

Jesus replied, "But even more blessed are all who hear the word of God and put it into practice." (Luke 11:28).

But don't just listen to God's word. You must do what it says. Otherwise, you are only fooling yourselves. For if you listen to the word and don't obey, it is like glancing at your face in the mirror. You see yourself, walk away, and forget what you look like. But if you look carefully into the perfect law that sets you free, and if you do what it says and don't forget what you heard, then God will bless you for doing it. (James 1:22-25).

4. OBEDIENCE TO GOD PROVES OUR LOVE

The books of 1 John and 2 John clearly explain that obedience to God demonstrates love for God. Loving God involves following his commands:

By this we know that we love the children of God, when we love God and obey his commandments. For this is the love of God, that we keep his commandments (1John 5:2-3).

Love means doing what God has commanded us, and he has commanded us to love one another, just as you heard from the beginning. (2 John 6).

5. OBEDIENCE TO GOD DEMONSTRATES OUR FAITH

When we obey God, we show our trust and faith in him.

And we can be sure that we know him if we obey is commandments. If someone claims, "I know God," but doesn't obey God's commandments, that person is a liar and is not living in the truth. But those who obey God's word truly show how completely they love him. That is how we know we are living in him. Those who say they live in God should live their lives as Jesus did. (1 John 2:3-6).

6. OBEDIENCE IS BETTER THAN SACRIFICE

The phrase "obedience is better than sacrifice," has often perplexed Christians. It can only be understood from an Old Testament perspective. The law required the Israelite people to offer sacrifices to God, but those sacrifices and offerings were never intended to take the place of obedience.

But Samuel replied, "What is more pleasing to the Lord: your burnt offerings and sacrifices or your obedience to his voice? Listen! Obedience is better than sacrifice, and submission is better than offering the fat of rams, Rebellion is as sinful as witchcraft, and stubbornness as bad as worshiping idols. So because you have rejected the command of the LORD, he has rejected you as king." (1 Samuel 15:22-23).

7. DISOBEDIENCE LEADS TO SIN AND DEATH

The disobedience of Adam brought sin and death into the world. This is the basis of the term "original sin." But Christ's perfect obedience restores fellowship with God for everyone who believes in him.

For as by the one man's (Adams's) disobedience the many were made sinner's, so by the one man's (Christ's) obedience the many will be made righteous. (Romans 5:19). For as in Adam all die, so also in Christ shall all be made alive. (1 Corinthians 15:22).

8. THROUGH OBEDIENCE, WE EXPERIENCE THE BLESSINGS OF HOLY LIVING

Only Jesus Christ is perfect, therefore, only he could walk in sinless, perfect obedience. But as we allow the Holy Spirit to transform us from within, we grow in holiness. This is known as the process of sanctification, which can also be described as spiritual growth. The more we read God's Word, spend time with Jesus, and allow the Holy Spirit to change us from within, the more we grow in obedience and holiness as Christians:

Joyful are people of integrity, who follow the instructions of the LORD, Joyful are those who obey his laws and search for him with all their hearts. They do not compromise with evil, and they walk only in his paths. You have charged us to keep your commandments carefully. Oh that my actions would consistently reflect your decrees! Then I will not be ashamed when I compare my life with your commands. As I learn your righteous regulations, I will thank you by living as I should! I will obey your decrees. Please don't give up on me! (Psalm 119:1-8).

Scriptures on Obedience

James 1:22-25	Deuteronomy 6:18	Joshua 22:5
Psalm 112:1	Psalm 143:10	Matthew 6:24
Exodus 19:5	John 14:21	Psalm 119:44
Hebrews 13:17	Leviticus 26:3-13	

Obedience Word Search

```
A S K A A J S L I W A L K O X
D Q U W D F V R C K N M G N C
A P U A N B N J E H M W L O O
M J T N B L K P J W O F S A M
Y A U M O E V O L Z A O Y H M
D P T R U S T O B L R R S C A
O L G G W S Q C I O O J D E N
G O I R O E C N S C Z V A R D
V H N V U D K P F U E A E I M
S K L Q I F L P P X B T K M E
E J O K K N I X J J V M Z N N
Y E H H X D G J K D H W I H T
A S P E N O C H S J E G V T S
O U I Z M Y U D U P B S D P E S
O S A R C W Z W I L L I N G A S
```

Commandments	Willing	Blessed	Living
Submit	Reward	Jesus	Choose
Voice	Trust	Love	Enoch
Walk	Noah	God	Adam

Reflection:

Reflect on your life and current situation. What areas or things in your life needs improvement?

_____
_____
_____
_____
_____
_____
_____
_____
_____
_____
_____
_____

Notes

Notes

Notes

CHAPTER THREE

Overcoming Hindrances

Isaiah 59:2, "But your iniquities have made a separation between you and your God, and your sins have hidden His face from you so that He will not hear."

Our walk and spiritual growth begins the moment we invite God into our hearts. It's about committing our lives to God and submitting our lives to the Spirit's leading. The level of commitment means our souls should be on fire. And with that fire comes the attitude of 'WE'RE ALL IN'. In truth, it really is an ALL or nothing kind of deal.

What are some things that can be hindering your spiritual growth and walking in your full God given potential?

2 Timothy 2:7, "For God has not given us a spirit of fear, but of power and of love and of a sound mind."

God always gives us what we need. Paul reminded Timothy that God didn't give him timidity he felt, that he came either from Timothy's own baggage or from the pit of hell itself. Instead God equipped him with love, power, and a sound mind.

Love: The relational ingredient that enables us to attract and connect with others.

Power: The courage and competence to get the job done.

Sound Mind: The perspective and wisdom to gasp a vision and take the right steps.

Because God has so equipped us, He instructs us to not be ashamed but share in the sufferings" (2 Timothy 1:8). God gave Timothy (and us!) everything needed to accomplish the job. He empowers us before He ever expects from us. He gives before He demands. We receive His competence before we receive His commands.

Spiritual Weakness

Spiritual weakness is a serious spiritual disease that affects the faith of any child of God. It creates spiritual numbness and insensitivity. It leads to backsliding and spiritual backwardness. Most Christians' spiritual batteries have gone empty if not dead. May your spiritual battery be recharged. The Lord called us to grow and excel from grace to grace; from glory to glory, and from strength to strength. (Psalm 84:7, 2, Cor. 3:18). Spiritual weakness deprives us from experiencing and enjoying the riches of His Glory. It makes us prey to the enemy. Continued spiritual exercises such as fasting, praying, Bible reading, and practical obedience are cures against spiritual weakness. Spiritual discipline will keep us strong and well in the presence of the Lord. Cultivate a practical and prayerful lifestyle. The more we do this, we will experience a closer relationship with the Lord. We will grow stronger in the power of His might. The more intimate we become with the Lord, the more dangerous we will become. The devil is afraid of believer's who are submissive to God. They are those that can resist the devil. He has no choice but to flee.

Prayer focus: *Pray against spiritual weakness*

- ❖ Do personal spiritual examination.
- ❖ How is your faith in the Lord?
- ❖ Pray against weakness.
- ❖ Pray against any arrow of doubts that tends to weaken your faith.
- ❖ What is taking the place of God in your life? Idolized objects, etc.?
- ❖ What is taking your time, attention, affection, possessions, time, values?
- ❖ Pray against idolatry and any forms of spiritual distraction.
- ❖ Pray for increased faith.
- ❖ Full reliance and dependence on the Lord.
- ❖ When we put God first, every other thing will fall in line.

Prayer points*

1. Lord, I pray that you increase my faith in you. Help me believe in your power to handle anything that comes my way in Jesus name (Luke 17:5-10).

2. Heavenly Father, I pray that my faith will increase and make a greater impact in the mighty name of Jesus Christ (Matthew 17:20).

3. Lord, I pray against the spirit of doubt and spiritual instability (Mark 11:23, Luke 12:29).

4. Lord, deliver me from the spirit of fear and anything that has the ability to paralyze my faith in Jesus Mighty name (Isaiah 43:1-2, Deut. 31:1-6).

5. Oh Lord, help me to grow strong in faith, power, and prayer (1 Samuel 2:21, Luke 1:80, 2:52).

6. Father, every mountain of impossibility standing against my spiritual growth and destiny, let it be removed in the mighty name of Jesus Christ (Zech. 4:1-7, Mark 11:23).

7. By the spirit and Word of the Lord, I will obtain good report before God in everything relating to life and godliness in the mighty name of Jesus Christ (Hebrew 11:2; Peter 1:3).

8. I command all demonic mirrors and monitoring gadgets against my spiritual life to be broken in the name of Jesus.

9. Lord, catapult my spiritual life to the mountain top.

10. I pull down any power fighting my ability to read and study the Word in Jesus name.

11. Any plan of the enemy to bring down my prayer life is sabotaged, in the name of Jesus.

12. Let the fire of the Holy Ghost revive my spiritual life, in Jesus' name.

13. Every evil spiritual padlock and chain hindering my spiritual growth, be roasted, in the name of Jesus.

14. I rebuke every spirit of spiritual deafness and blindness to Your Word in my life, in the name of Jesus.

15. Let my spiritual eyes and ears be wide open, in the name of Jesus.

16. In the name of Jesus, I capture every power behind all my spiritual blindness and deafness.

17. I pray Lord, ignite my prayer life with Your fire in Jesus name.

18. I rebuke the spirit of laziness to my prayer life in Jesus name.

19. Let me be filled with all wisdom and spiritual understanding, in the name of Jesus.

20. Lord help me to walk worthy of, and pleasing to the Lord, in the name of Jesus.

21. Lord, make me be fruitful in every good work, in Jesus' name.

22. Lord, increase me in the knowledge of God to overcome any spirit of ignorance in my life in Jesus name.

23. I command any attack on my calling to scatter by fire, in the name of Jesus.

24. I bind the strongman stopping me from winning souls in the mighty name of Jesus.

25. Any idol taking away my devotion to God, receive fire in Jesus name.

26. Forces that are preventing my roots in Christ to go deeper be vanquished in Jesus name.

27. Lord let me be filled with all the fullness of God.

HINDRANCES TO SPIRITUAL GROWTH

(1) Lack of Prayer

Lack of an effective prayer life can lead to lack of direction and discernment in one's life. Prayer is not one-way. Prayer is two way communication with God

Therefore prayer is not only an opportunity for us to talk to God but prayer is also an opportunity for God to speak to us. God hears us and we hear God.

We draw spiritually close to the Lord by spending more time with Him.

<u>Jeremiah 33:3</u> – *"Call to Me, and I will answer you, and show you great and mighty things, which you do not know."*

1 Thessalonians 5:17 – *"Pray without ceasing."*

James 5:16 – *"Confess your trespasses to one another, and pray for one another, that you may be healed. The effective, fervent prayer of a righteous man avails much."*

(2) Lack of Bible Study & Meditation

Another hindrance to spiritual growth is when a person does not study and meditate on the word of God. Through the studying of the Scriptures we learn

   a. The divine nature of God

   b. The plans and precepts of God

   c. The sinful nature of man & God's redemption for man through Jesus Christ

   d. The nature of mankind's enemy and how the enemy is defeated through Christ

   e. God's spiritual guidelines for godly living.

2 Timothy 2:15 – *"Be diligent to present yourself approved to God, a worker who does not need to be ashamed, rightly dividing the word of truth".*

Joshua 1:8 – *"This Book of the Law shall not depart from your mouth, but you shall meditate in it day and night, that you may observe to do according to all that is written in it. For then you will make your way prosperous, and then you will have good success."*

<u>**Hebrews 4:12**</u>– *"For the word of God is living and powerful, and sharper than any two-edged sword, piercing even to the division of soul and spirit, and of joints and marrow, and is a discerner of the thoughts and intents of the heart".*

(3) Lack of Fellowship With Other Believers

Without fellowship with the right people, it can be difficult to grow spiritually.

When you have the right people around you, such people edify, build and encourage you in the Lord.

Fellowship with unbelievers can lead to backsliding and spiritual corruption. It's therefore important to guard yourself against the wrong kind of influences as you grow in your Christian faith.

<u>**1 Corinthians 15:33**</u> – *Do not be deceived: "Evil company corrupts good habits".*

<u>**2 Corinthians 6:14, 15**</u>– *"Do not be unequally yoked together with unbelievers. For what fellowship has righteousness with lawlessness? And what communion has light with darkness? 15 And what accord has Christ with Belial? Or what part has a believer with an unbeliever?"*

(4) Listening to Bad / False Doctrine

False doctrine can hinder spiritual growth. When a person spiritually feeds himself with the wrong information, such doctrine will corrupt the person. God warns us through his word against obeying false doctrine and also He warns us to avoid following false prophets. A person who follows false doctrine and false teachers is a person who is not only deceived – but that person also deceives himself.

Matthew 24:11 – *"Then many false prophets will rise up and deceive many."*

1 Timothy 4:1 – *"Now the Spirit expressly says that in latter times some will depart from the faith, giving heed to deceiving spirits and doctrines of demons."*

1 Timothy 4:16 – *"Take heed to yourself and to the doctrine. Continue in them, for in doing this you will save both yourself and those who hear you."*

(5) Living in Sin

A life of unconfessed sin is a hindrance to spiritual growth. When a person does not feel conviction when he sins or when he/she is not repentant of a sinful habit that sin can stagnate that person's growth in the Lord.

It's therefore important to always confess our sins. We must also forgive our neighbor if our neighbor has offended us. We must walk in love and humility.

Pride is the root cause of many sins.

Isaiah 59:1-2 – *"Behold, the Lord's hand is not shortened, That it cannot save; Nor His ear heavy, That it cannot hear. 2 But your iniquities have separated you from your God; And your sins have hidden His face from you, So that He will not hear."*

1 John 1:9 – *"If we confess our sins, He is faithful and just to forgive us our sins and to cleanse us from all unrighteousness."*

Are you growing? If not, seek the Lord; read His word; spend time in prayer; remove the obstacles in your life that prevent or stagnate your walk with the Lord. Surrender all to God.

Notes

Notes

Notes

CHAPTER FOUR

Faith In The Word

*"Now **faith** is the substance of things hoped for, the evidence of things not seen"*
Hebrew 11:1.

Having faith means recognizing that you have no control, that what will be, will be and that there is a greater power, whether it be God or the universe.

People in the Bible who showed exceptional faith:

1. Abraham was known as the father of faith and a friend to God. God promised Abraham he was going to be the father of many nations. Abraham and Sarah was in their old age. They had faith in God, so God gave them a child called Isaac. Many years have passed; however, Abraham still knew God was going to do what He promised. The Bible says he was fully convicted, even when Sarah doubted God. Abraham knew without faith it is impossible to please God. For he that cometh to God must believe that he is, and that he is a rewarder of them that diligently seek him. (Hebrew 11:6).

2. The women with the issue of blood.-Mark 5:25-34. "A woman in the crowd had suffered for twelve years with constant bleeding. She had heard about Jesus, so she came up behind Him through the crowd and touched His robe.

For she thought to herself, "If I can just touch His robe, I will be healed." Immediately the bleeding stopped, and she could feel in her body that she had been healed of her terrible condition. Then the frightened woman, trembling at the realization of what had happened to her, cam e and fell to her knees in front of Him and told Him and what she had done. And he said to her, 'Daughter, your faith has made you well. Go in peace. Your suffering is over." Having faith is believing in the Word of God in-spite of what things look like in the natural. Faith is having hope during difficult times.

Faith is a firm conviction. When you have a firm conviction you can stand your ground and refuse to allow your faith in God to be shaken. Therefore, you can stand fast and refuse to be moved by what anyone else says, or by medical reports. It is a matter of taking God at His Word.

QUESTION: How can we live in a way that impacts the World for Christ without allowing the World to impact us?

When learning how to be in the world but not of the world; when we don't make decisions based on fleshly leading.

Example: I knew I needed to avoid the St. Patrick's Day celebrations because the only motivating factors were fleshly. We definitely shouldn't head into questionable situations when it's our flesh that's leading us there!

As an alternative to the parties, I ended up initiating a small get together with a group of Christian friends for Bible study and prayer.

Example: If you have a friend who invites you to a party at another friend's house and you know that they will be serving alcohol, which is against your moral values, the wise decision is to not attend.

An alternative would be to invite your friend to a cookout surrounding other Christians and fellowshipping.

What are the five kinds of faith?

1. <u>Saving Faith</u> – Ephesians 2:8 "For by grace are you saved through faith; and that not of yourselves; it is the gift of God."

Saving faith is the faith God imparts to the believer for salvation. It is a gift as none of us had faith unless God first bestows it upon us. It is by this faith that we enter the kingdom of God. When we come to the cross and see our sins and we reach out to God, He reaches down to us and gives us faith to receive Jesus Christ as our Lord and Savior.

2. <u>The Fruit of Faith</u> – One fruit of the Spirit is "faith" **(**Galatians 5:22-23). Some bible translations say "faithfulness" but it is "faith." This fruit of faith is the one we use for living the Christian life. This faith is called "the faith of righteousness" for the bible says "The righteous shall live by faith and not by sight" (Romans 1:17). This faith comes by the indwelling presence of the Holy Spirit and must become part of our character as we walk in the Spirit.

3. <u>The Measure of Faith</u> – Romans 12:3 "For I say, through the grace given to me, to everyone who is among you, not to think of himself more highly than he ought to think, but to think soberly, as God has dealt to each one a measure of faith."

This measure of faith is the faith God gives us by His grace to minister our spiritual gifts to other and do what he has called us to do. It takes faith to be used by God!

4. Mountain Moving Faith – Mark 11:23 "Whoever says to this mountain, 'Be removed and cast into the sea' and does not doubt in his heart, but believes that those things he says will come to pass, he will have whatever he says."

Mountain moving faith is great faith. It the faith that causes us to move the mountains that stand in the way of God's promises, will and purpose for our lives. This type of faith will produce the greater works Jesus spoke about. Mega faith!

Lastly, we have....

5. The Gift of Faith – 1 Corinthians 12:4a, 9a "Now there are diversities of gifts... to another faith by the same Spirit."

This type of faith is a special impartation that comes from the Holy Spirit to believe God for a specific work or circumstance. This is the faith that kicks in when your faith can go no further. This gift of faith begins where your faith ends. When you receive this type of faith, you feel as though you are being carried by God. It is no longer your faith, it's God's faith. This type of faith does not necessarily have to be a great faith; it can be faith for small things as well. It is a gift of the Holy Spirit.

What is your level of faith ?...

Bible knowledge quiz

True faith is demonstrated in good deeds?	True or False
Works don't lead to, make, or take the place of faith?	True or False
Heaven is the object of true faith?	True or False
An evidence of God's blessing for faith is seen in Caleb receiving land in Hebron as promised 40 years earlier?	True or False
Faith brings things of God from the spiritual realm into the physical realm?	True or False
Faith make things happen?	True or False
Faith is taking Jesus at his word?	True or False
Abraham faith was wavering?	True or False
Faith in God is the greatest strength?	True or False
Our faith increases as we look to God during trials?	True or False

Heroes of Faith

11 Now faith is the reality of what is hoped for, the proof of what is not seen. ² For our ancestors won God's approval by it.

³ By faith we understand that the universe was created by God's command, so that what is seen has been made from things that are not visible.

⁴ By faith Abel offered to God a better sacrifice than Cain did. By faith he was approved as a righteous man, because God approved his gifts, and even though he is dead, he still speaks through his faith.

⁵ By faith Enoch was taken away so he did not experience death, and he was not to be found because God took him away. For prior to his removal he was approved, since he had pleased God. ⁶ Now without faith it is impossible to please God, for the one who draws near to Him must believe that He exists and rewards those who seek Him.

⁷ By faith Noah, after he was warned about what was not yet seen and motivated by godly fear, built an ark to deliver his family. By faith he condemned the world and became an heir of the righteousness that comes by faith.

⁸ By faith Abraham, when he was called, obeyed and went out to a place he was going to receive as an inheritance. He went out, not knowing where he was going. ⁹ By faith he stayed as a foreigner in the land of promise, living in tents with Isaac and Jacob, coheirs of the same promise. ¹⁰ For he was looking forward to the city that has foundations, whose architect and builder is God.

¹¹ By faith even Sarah herself, when she was unable to have children, received power to conceive offspring, even though she was past the age, since she considered that the One who had promised was faithful. ¹² Therefore from one man—in fact, from one as good as dead—came offspring as numerous as the stars of heaven and as innumerable as the grains of sand by the seashore.

¹³ These all died in faith without having received the promises, but they saw them from a distance, greeted them, and confessed that they were foreigners and temporary residents on the earth. ¹⁴ Now those who say such things make it clear that they are seeking a homeland. ¹⁵ If they were thinking about where they came from, they would have had an opportunity to return. ¹⁶ But they now desire a better place—

a heavenly one. Therefore God is not ashamed to be called their God, for He has prepared a city for them.

[17] By faith Abraham, when he was tested, offered up Isaac. He received the promises and he was offering his unique son, [18] the one it had been said about, Your seed will be traced through Isaac. [19] He considered God to be able even to raise someone from the dead, and as an illustration, he received him back.

[20] By faith Isaac blessed Jacob and Esau concerning things to come. [21] By faith Jacob, when he was dying, blessed each of the sons of Joseph, and he worshiped, leaning on the top of his staff. [22] By faith Joseph, as he was nearing the end of his life, mentioned the exodus of the Israelites and gave instructions concerning his bones.

[23] By faith, after Moses was born, he was hidden by his parents for three months, because they saw that the child was beautiful, and they didn't fear the king's edict. [24] By faith Moses, when he had grown up, refused to be called the son of Pharaoh's daughter [25] and chose to suffer with the people of God rather than to enjoy the short-lived pleasure of sin. [26] For he considered the reproach because of the Messiah to be greater wealth than the treasures of Egypt, since his attention was on the reward.

[27] By faith he left Egypt behind, not being afraid of the king's anger, for Moses persevered as one who sees Him who is invisible. [28] By faith he instituted the Passover and the sprinkling of the blood, so that the destroyer of the firstborn might not touch the Israelites. [29] By faith they crossed the Red Sea as though they were on dry land. When the Egyptians attempted to do this, they were drowned.

[30] By faith the walls of Jericho fell down after being encircled by the Israelites for seven days. [31] By faith Rahab the prostitute received the spies in peace and didn't perish with those who disobeyed. (Hebrews 1-30).

What are some challenges that you faced in your life that tested your faith? And how did you handle it? Explain.

Notes

Notes

Notes

CHAPTER FIVE

Prayer

Luke 18:1, "And he spake a parable unto them to this end, that men aught always to pray, and not to faint."

Prayer is a communication process that allows us to talk to God, a solemn request for help or expression of thanks addressed to God.

Types Of Prayer

1. **Prayer of Agreement:** (Matthew18:19), "Again I say unto you, that if two of you shall agree on earth as touching anything that they shall as, it shall be done for them of my Father which is in Heaven."

2. **Prayer of Faith:** (Mark 11:24), "Therefore I say unto you, whatever things you ask when you pray, believe that you receive them, and will have them."

3. **Prayer of Consecration and Dedication:** (Luke 22:42), "Saying Father, if thou be willing, remove this cup from me: nevertheless not my will, but thine be done." This is prayer committing your life and will to God.

4. **Prayer of Praise & Worship:** (Luke 2:20), "Then the shepherds returned, glorifying and praising God for all the things they had heard and see, as it was told them." You enter into God's presence with worship and praise:

"Enter into His gates with thanksgiving, and into His courts with praise; be thankful unto Him, and bless His Name" (Psalm 100:4).

Worship is the giving of honor and devotion. Praise is thanksgiving and an expression of gratitude not only for what God has done but for who He is. You are to worship God in Spirit and in Truth.

"But the hour cometh, and now is, when the true worshipers shall worship the Father in Spirit and in truth: for the Father seeketh such to worship Him. God is a Spirit, and they that worship Him must worship Him in spirit and in truth" (John 4:23-24).

Praise and Worship can be with:

Singing:	Psalms 9:2,11: 40:3; Mark 14:26
Audible Praise:	Psalms 103:1
Shouting:	Psalms 47:1
Lifting up of the hands:	Psalms 63:4; 134:2; 1 Timothy 2:8
Clapping:	Psalms 47:1
Musical Instruments:	Psalms 150:3-5
Standing:	II Chronicles 20:19
Bowing:	Psalms 95:6
Dancing:	Psalms 149:3
Kneeling	Psalms 95:6
Lying Down	Psalms 149:5

5. **<u>Prayer of Intercession</u>:** (Philippians 1:3-4), "I thank my God upon every remembrance of you, always in every prayer of mine for you all making request with joy." Intercession is praying for others. An intercessor is one who takes the place of another or pleads another's case.

6. **Prayer of Binding & Loosing:** (Matthew 18:18), "Verily I say unto you, whatsoever ye shall bind on earth shall be bound in heaven: and whatsoever ye shall loose on earth shall be loosed in heaven."

7. **Petition:** Prayers of petition are requests. Requests must be made according to the will of God. As revealed in His written Word. Petitions may be at the levels of asking, seeking, or knocking. Supplication is another word for this type of prayer. The word supplication means "beseeching God or strongly appealing to Him in behalf of a need.

8. **Confession and Repentance:** A prayer of confession is repenting and asking forgiveness for sin.

"If we confess our sins, He is faithful and just to forgive us our sins and to cleanse us from all unrighteousness" (1 John 1:9).

Hindrances to Effective Intercession

Sin, backsliding	Unbelief
Not asking in Jesus name	Pride, hypocrisy
Power hungry, manipulation	Works of flesh
Unforgiveness	Soulish Blockages
Doubt	Lust
Worry	Lack of tithing
Lack of faith	Disobedience
Not abiding in the Word	Hardened heart, bitterness
Offense	Rebellion
Satanic activities	Idols

True or False

1. The prayer of adoration is taking a long, loving look at God? _____

2. For the Christian, life is a Gift? _____

3. Prayers that express gratitude to God are _____ called prayers of Adoration?

4. Prayers of intercession are prayers for all people _____ except for our enemies?

5. We can always find something for which to give God Praise? _____

6. Communication is a two way street? _____

7. Jesus teaches us to pray in his name? _____

8. One can achieve intimacy with God without learning _____ to listen to God?

9. God's message or revelation is shown to us in many _____ ways including creation and scripture?

10. Living a holy life and dancing are almost total opposites? _____

11. We should only pray when times are tough? _____

12. We should pray without ceasing? _____

13. Prayer helps us to grow stronger in faith? _____

14. Prayer is a lifestyle? _____

15. Jesus was our model for prayer and fasting? _____

How to act When Praying

GOD knows who you are. So when you pray, be yourself. Be sincere. Be respectful, but most importantly, remember that prayer is a conversation.

Sitting or standing?

Traditionally, individual prayer means kneeling with arms folded and eyes closed. But people throughout the scriptures prayed when standing (1 Kings 8:22), when sitting down, or when kneeling (Luke 22:41). People pray when prostrate, with hands raised, with eyes closed, and with eyes lifted up. God is concerned less with how you pray than that you are praying in the first place.

Out loud or in silence

Because it is a conversation, prayer is usually expressed out loud. But you can pray in silence too. When people in the Book of Mormon were threatened with death if caught praying, they "did not raise their voices to the Lord their God, but did pour out their hearts to him; and he did know the thoughts of their minds" (Mosiah 24:12).

How long should I pray?

Jesus "continued all night in prayer to God" (Luke 6:12) when selecting His disciples. Enos, a prophet in the book of Mormon, prayed "all the day long" and into the night when he was asking for forgiveness from sins (Enos 1:4). But the length of your prayer is less important than always having a prayer I your heart. "I pray continually for my people by day, and mine eyes water my pillow by night…and I cry unto my God in faith, and I know that he will hear my cry" (2 Nephi 33:3).

How do I listen for an answer?

God hears and answers every prayer. He is listening. You should listen too. Take time after your prayer to ponder the conversation. Sometimes when you are feeling especially close to God, you may feel a sense of inner warmth or peace. This is the Holy Spirit. It is one of the ways you can experience answers to your prayers. Remember, listening to God is an important part of prayer. Be aware of feelings you have, especially of peace. Answers to prayers often come as thoughts or ideas in your mind. Scriptures may come to your mind because they hold greater personal meaning and answers. Be willing to accept or act on the answer God chooses to give.

The Lord's Prayer

Our Father, who is in heaven,

Hallowed be Your name,

Your Kingdom come,

Your will be done,

On earth, as it is in heaven,

Give us each day our daily bread,

And forgive us our sins,

For we also forgive everyone who is indebted to us,

And lead us not into temptation, but deliver us from the evil one,

For thine is the Kingdom, the Power, and the Glory

Forever and ever Amen

Luke 11:2-4

Life In Christ Workbook

Type of Prayer

```
B E N E D I C T I O N C I
N R W J M L P H B M O M N
O Z P W F B F E L M J R T
I N K E K K S R M K M P E
S R L Z T I R I N N J H R
S G K P A I T J V R B H C
E W L R F M T T B J K N E
F R P B E R D I X W G Z S
N C Z N D N T Y O R T N S
O D T X K N N L K N V J I
C K N H K B M V M F L F O
T S S E N E V I G R O F N
T H A N K S G I V I N G K
```

www.churchhousepuzzles.com © 2011

Benediction

Commitment

Confession

Forgiveness

Intercession

Petition

Praise

Thanksgiving

58

The Names Of God

Adoni- Lord, Master (Genesis 15:2)

El Elyon- The Most High God (Genesis 14:18-20)

El Olam- The Everlasting God (Isaiah 40:28-31)

El Roi- The Strong One Who Sees (Genesis 16:13)

El Shaddai- Lord God Almighty (Genesis 17:1)

Elohim- God of Power and Might (Genesis 1:1)

Jehovah Jireh- (The Lord Will Provide Genesis 22:13-14)

Jehovah Mekoddishkem- The Lord Who Sanctifies You (Exodus 31:13)

Jehovah Nissi- The Lord My Banner/Victory (Exodus 17:15)

Jehovah Raah- The Lord My Shepherd (Psalm 23:1)

Jehovah Rapha- The Lord That Heals (Exodus 15:26)

Jehovah Sabaoth- The Lord Of Hosts (Isaiah 1:24)

Jehovah Shalom- The Lord is Peace (Judges 6:24)

Jehovah Shammah- The Lord is There/Present (Ezekiel 48:35)

Jehovah Tsidkenu- The Lord Our Righteousness (Jeremiah 23:6)

Yahweh- Lord, Jehovah (Deuteronomy 6:4)

Qanna- Jealous God (Exodus 20:5)

Ephesians 6:20

Notes

Notes

Notes

CHAPTER SIX.

Victoriously Living

Matthew 17:21, "But this kind does not go out except by prayer and fasting."

God desires His children to live victoriously. Victorious means: triumphant, conquering or having won the victory over something.

Genesis 4:7, "If you do well, shall you not be accepted? But if you do not do well, sin is crouching at the door. It desires to dominate you, but you must rule over it."

God wants us to have victory over life's challenges.

Romans 8:35-39, "Who shall separate us from the love of Messiah? Shall tribulation, or distress, or persecution, or famine, or nakedness, or pencil, or sword? As it is written:

"For Your sake we are killed all day long; we are counted as sheep for the slaughter." No, in all these things we are more than conquerors through Him who loved us. For I am persuaded that neither death nor life, neither angels nor principalities nor power, neither things present nor things to come, neither height nor depth, nor any other created thing, shall be able to separate us from the love of God, which is in Messiah Yeshua our Lord."

It is persevering through trouble, hardship, persecution, famine, nakedness, danger, or sword. We are to live with our eyes set on the things of Heaven, not of this World. Jesus is our model in this.

- ❖ The victorious Christian is faithful. (Hebrews 11:1)
- ❖ The victorious Christian makes spiritual progress.
- ❖ Victorious over the World, Lust of the flesh, lust of the eyes, and the pride of life (1 John 2:16).
- ❖ Conquering of fear knowing Gods peace (John 14:27)
- ❖ Defeat of death itself (1 Corinthians 15:54-55)
- ❖ Dealing with temptation (1 Corinthians 10:13)
- ❖ Jesus is the vine (John 15)
- ❖ Journey of faith, eternal salvation (Galatians 2:20)

Five Keys to Victorious Living

<u>WATCH-</u> To be alert, be ready and on guard (Used in connection with prayer)

1. Watch for the adversary (1 Peter 5:8-9)
2. Watch for wolves (Acts 20: 28-31)
3. Watch for one another (Ephesians 6:18)
4. Watch for the return of the Lord (Matthew 24:42-44)
5. Be brave and courageous (Philippians 1:27-28)

True or False

1. A Victorious Christian is one who seeks God and desires to please Him?   True or False
2. The key to living victoriously is to have faith in God's Word? True or False

3. One can live in disobedience and live a victorious life?   True or False

4. Victorious living requires helping others in need and giving of yourself? True or False

5. We are to live in the world and worship other gods? True or False

6. We are to give of our tithes once and a while? True or False

7. God created us as a reflection of Jesus Christ here on the earth? True or False

8. Victorious living is putting on the full armor of God? True or False

9. We are to pray for others and declare the Word of God? True or False

10. We are to stay connected to the vine which is God in Heaven? True or False

11. We are indwelled with the Holy Spirit who empowers us? True or False

12. Faith gives us conviction and trust to stand strong against temptations? True or False

13. We grow in faith as we get closer to God?   True or False

We have the victory through Christ Jesus!

Master over sin, Genesis 4:7

Victory song, Exodus 15:1-18

Assured victory, Deuteronomy 3:2

Yours to conquer, Joshua 8:1

We won, 2 Samuel 18:28

Resource in time of weakness, 2 Chronicles 14:11

VICTORY

Oh what a joy to know that we have the victory!

Jesus paid it all for us on the cross at Calvary

I am honored to know that he loves us so much

When I worship him, I can feel his touch

There is no place in this World that I would rather be

But in the arms of the one who gave me victory

I cherish the times I have at hand

Uniting with others in our land

When times get tough I turn to Jesus

Because he is the only one who can free us

He took on our burdens so we can live

A wonderful life, what a great joy this is

Thank you Jesus for this wonderful gift!

I will praise you forever, Hallelujah Amen!

Poem by Michelle Fortune

Join a Church

Matthew 16:18, "And I tell you Peter, and on this rock I will build my church, and the gates of Hades will not overcome it."

Jesus established the church to be public, earthly institution that would mark out, affirm, and oversee those who profess to believe in him.

Why is it important to join a church?

- ❖ Display of the good news about Jesus.
- ❖ Fellowship with other believers who are strong in the faith.
- ❖ Empowerment.
- ❖ Encouragement and edification.
- ❖ Helps new believers grow close to God and in His Word.
- ❖ Helps us to connect with other likeminded Christians.
- ❖ Unity, Power & Prayer

Church Connects Us With God

There is something reverent about simply being inside a church. It gives us a physical space to connect and draw closer to God and to realize that there is something out there bigger than ourselves.

Plus entering a house of worship, we're instantly elevated to a state where we're opening ourselves to God and trying to understand his message. The simple act of walking in the door brings you closer. Ultimately, that connection with God is strengthened and reinforced by church attendance. We're making time for God and physically allowing him into our lives by attending a place of worship.

Church Gives Us A Chance To Reflect On Gratitude

By practicing gratitude, we can reframe negative or frustrating situations into learning opportunities. Gratitude helps us to realize how blessed we are and how much we truly have. Even when things seem dire and awful (say, your husband lost his job, your child is sick, or a loved one passes away), church helps us change our outlook and stop dwelling on empty questions like, "Why is this happening to me?"

Church can help us realize the things we do have, even when we feel lost. For example, we may have access to modern medical care for our sick child, a network of people to support and help our spouse during a job search, or memories and lessons we hold on to from our time with our loved one, as well as the prospect of reuniting with them in heaven. Even if it's hard to see the blessings at the moment, attending church can help us open our hearts and eyes to see the things we have.

Church Connects Us Socially

A more peripheral benefit of church attendance is the way it connects us socially. This is especially true if you have recently moved to a new town, or even just a new neighborhood. As a general rule, church people are pretty friendly, and most churches have a variety of social events, groups, clubs, and connection opportunities available each week. If you're struggling to meet people or to make friends, this is the place to do it!

Church Helps Us Better Connect With Our Spouse

Not everyone is on the same page as his or her spouse when it comes to faith. However, couples who attend church together report higher levels of happiness and satisfaction within their marriage. Why is that? Church reconnects us to our shared beliefs. It reinforces the higher philosophy and purpose behind marriage and family, and it allows us a safe space to connect with God and our spouse together.

Couples who attend church together are making time to reiterate the important foundations of their marriage. When you got married, you pledged to love and support each other. When you commune with God at church on Sundays, you're reminded of your pledge and your connection is reinforced.

Church Allows Us To Feel Reverence

In the chaos of every day, do you ever long for peace, quiet and reverence? When we attend church, we're transported to a place of worship and peace. I'm always amazed at the peaceful feeling that washes over me the moment I walk into the building. It's a place of calm and a place of joy.

Attending church can help us revisit this revered state regularly. It gives us a space to pray and to express humility and gratitude. It allows us to feel at peace and gives us respite from the hustle and bustle of our daily lives.

Church Provides Plenty Of Opportunities To Give Back

Most Christian churches offer some type of charity work and assistance for their communities and other areas of need around the world. Through our faith, we've been able to visit and help communities around the world, as well as locally in a variety of ways.

Church offers an opportunity to donate our time and money to causes we believe in. We can also help out through organizations who share the same values and want to share God's Grace and love with those in need. We're so blessed to live full lives with so much opportunity, safety and freedom. So many people in the world live in poverty and pain, and through our faith, we can help bring them comfort and help.

Church Helps Us "Find the Lesson" In Our Trials

A friend of mine was recently struggling because, try as she might, she and her husband couldn't get to stable financial ground. It made her heartsick to have to work full-time when she was desperately longing to stay home with her young child. She said, "I'm having such a hard time figuring out what I'm supposed to learn from this experience."

It's such a normal response, isn't it? We all want to know why things don't always go the way we planned.

But I can't even tell you how many times I've been struggling in a particular area and found that the sermon or message applied so directly to my situation, that it felt like the pastor was talking directly to me. Church helps us "get it," whether we are ready for it or not.

Church Teaches Us Forgiveness

It can be hard to let go of disappointments, frustrations, and annoyances. Maybe a friend has let us down, our kids have been out of control lately, or our spouse has said or done something hurtful. Forgiveness is one of the **hardest lessons** to learn, and yet, when are finally able to let things go, it can take a huge weight off our shoulders.

There's no better place to be reminded of the gift of forgiveness that we have already received, than by going to church, and our hearts can help but be softened in the process.

Church Fills Our Hearts With Song

There's something a little bit magical about music. Listening to hymns and religious music can uplift us, and give us messages we may not otherwise hear. It's amazing how open our hearts can become through song, and how sometimes even the weight of the world can be lifted off our shoulders, the moment that first song begins playing.

Through music, we feel more spiritually connected because song is a conduit to God. We can feel joy and happiness by listening to music with a great message, then carrying that song in our hearts all week long.

Church Is Where We Find Deeper Meaning In Our Lives

In my most frustrated and stressed-out moments, I sometimes find myself wondering, "What's the point?" When we feel despair, sorrow, frustration, and stress, it's easy to lose sight of the greater plan and purpose that's out there for all of us. We might even feel alone and isolated from God and from other people.

But when we go to church, we're given a greater sense of purpose and meaning. We can see the history of what has led us up to this point, and the promise that lies in our future even beyond this world. Church helps us revisit the larger narrative of life and the reasons to hold on and keep the faith.

The next time you're feeling like church might be more stress than it's worth, remind yourself it's a sign you NEED church in your life even more! Church can help alleviate our stress, ease our burdens and carry us through the week-something we all need.

Be A Cheerful Giver

2 Corinthians 9:7, "Each of you should give what you have decided in your heart to give, not reluctantly or under compulsion, for God loves a cheerful giver."

When we give generously and with a willing heart, God assures us He will watch over us and provide for us. His blessings will rain down upon us, abundantly and overflowing.

The Cheerful Giver

The point is this: whoever sows sparingly will also reap sparingly, and whoever sows bountifully will also reap bountifully. Each one must give as he has decided in his heart, not reluctantly or under compulsion, for God loves a cheerful giver.

10 Reasons Why God Loves A Cheerful Giver

Giving should be cause for joy for all believers, but many people become defensive or give excuses when asked to give or avoid the subject altogether. Here are 10 biblical reasons we should give with full and joyful hearts.

#1 God loves it when we give

2 Corinthians 9:7 says…

"Each one must give as he has decided in his heart, not reluctantly or under compulsion, for God loves a cheerful giver."

There are numerous places in Scripture where giving is commanded, and generous giving was actually written into the early law of the Hebrews. However, the reasons for giving were not arbitrary: the Israelites were commanded to give out of gratitude for God's provision.

In the New Testament, the church was instructed to give with that same joy. There are biblical precedents and legitimate arguments for structured giving (like tithing), but at its core, our giving should come from a joyful heart that recognizes God as the One Who first gave us so much.

That joy should permeate our every gift.

#2 We should give expecting God to provide

Jesus says in Luke 6:38…

"Give, and it will be given to you. Good measure, pressed down, shaken together, running over, will be put into your lap. For with the measure you use it will be measured back to you."

This statement of Jesus is not an endorsement of the prosperity gospel, which teaches that doing good for others will automatically result in tangible blessings from God. However, Jesus does say that our giving to others will be answered with God's abundant provision. It may not translate directly into dollar signs, but our blessing for faithful obedience to God will always be greater than we could ask or imagine.

#3 Our giving is to be considered a worthy sacrifice to God

Romans 12:1 says…

"I appeal to you therefore, brothers, by the mercies of God, to present your bodies as a living sacrifice, holy and acceptable to God, which is your spiritual worship."

Giving is not limited to our money or our possessions. We are to give our very bodies and lives in worship to God. Because Christ's sacrifice on the cross saved us and brought us back into a right relationship with God, we should be overjoyed to return our lives to His service. This is the truest form of worship, and giving of our time and energies is equally as beneficial to those around us as writing a check.

#4 The heart of the giver can matter more than the size of the gift

Luke 21:1-4 says…

"Jesus looked up and saw the rich putting their gifts into the offering box, and He saw a poor widow put in two small copper coins. And He said, 'Truly, I tell you, this poor widow has put in more than all of them. For they all contributed out of their abundance, but she out of her poverty put in all she had to live on.'"

Jesus recognized that the woman's gift, though small in amount, was great in faith. She gave a greater proportion of her income than the rich Pharisees, and her gift was considered acceptable to the Son of God. Jesus talked more about money than He did about any other topic during Hisrecorded ministry. This was, not surprisingly, because the culture He lived in was so preoccupied with giving only when it looked good to others, or when the gift was large enough to be worthy of recognition. We face similar pressures today.

#5 Be content with the basics, give away the rest

1 Timothy 6:8 says…

"But if we have food and clothing, with these we will be content."

This can help us learn the right way to look at our finances. If our basic needs are covered, and we have the ability to give out of our relative abundance, we should be content that God has provided and be the mechanism by which others can have their own needs met. God wants to use us to bless others. If we have extra funds available and would ordinarily only use them on ourselves, we should consider ways to use that money as an offering to God through the church or some other charitable group.

#6 Our giving can be a measurement of our faith

Malachi 3:10 says…

"Bring the full tithe into the storehouse, that there may be food in My house. And thereby put Me to the test, says the LORD of hosts, if I will not open the windows of heaven for you and pour down for you a blessing until there is no more need."

Some people hold back from giving when things get tough: your raise didn't come through, or you lost your job completely. According to the wisdom of the world, it would certainly make sense to stop tithing or giving to the church and save as much money as possible to take care of our families. We should certainly be responsible stewards of what God has given us, but that must first mean that we return a portion back to God through our giving. God will see our faith in tithing and giving, and answer our trust in His ability to provide abundant blessings.

There are so many stories of people going through hardship that still tithe and serve others with their money, and their needs are more than met. Rather than simply relying on yourself, trust that

God will take care of you in every way – and when He does, you can acknowledge Him with confidence and peace.

#7 Giving is an outward sign of our love for others

1 John 3:17 says…

"But if anyone has the world's goods and sees his brother in need, yet closes his heart against him, how does God's love abide in him?"

This is a straightforward and honest assessment of those who claim to love others but do not do what they can to help them. There are no specific conditions or stipulations laid down here, simply a matter of the heart. If you know of someone in need but refuse to help them even though you are more than capable of doing so, that is an act of selfishness. You may not be able to do much, but even the little you have can be an enormous blessing to others and a tremendous witness for the Gospel.

#8 Our giving allows us to serve God better

2 Corinthians 9:8 says…

"And God is able to make all grace abound to you, so that having all sufficiency in all things at all times, you may abound in every good work."

The Apostle Paul follows us his statement that "God loves a cheerful giver" with a promise that is made to all givers. God will graciously provide us everything we need, not simply so that we are content with our material comforts, but that we are further equipped to do even more good works. Our gifts and our blessings are not meant to be hoarded and kept away from others.

We have been given much so that we can give much away. That is the spirit of God's giving to us, and that is how we should freely give to others.

#9 Our giving should be rooted in love

1 Corinthians 13:3 says…

"If I give away all I have, and if I deliver up my body to be burned, but have not love, I gain nothing."

This verse helps to open the famous "love chapter" of the Bible in 1 Corinthians. Buried in this passage, however, is an important lesson about giving. God loves a cheerful giver, not one who gives, but doesn't care how or why they give. We can give away all we own, and even give up our very lives; but if love is not our primary motivation for giving, it is an empty gift. Whoever you choose to give to, be sure that love is behind our every gift.

#10 Greed can lead to our downfall

Proverbs 28:27 says…

"Whoever gives to the poor will not want, but he who hides his eyes will get many a curse."

Taken on its own, this can seem like a harsh indictment toward possessions of any kind.

However, it is important to recognize that the problem is turning away from those in need.

If we give freely we are blessed by God – if not in material blessings returned to us, then through

God's love being shined out through our lives. However, if we turn a blind eye to the needs of others, we are in essence denying our responsibility to be the hands and feet of Jesus in this world. We are called to be responsible stewards of the money and possessions that God has given us, but we are also commanded to be joyously generous. The next time you have the opportunity to give, do so with a full and open heart, seeing the God of love and provision behind your gift.

Notes

Notes

Notes

CHAPTER SEVEN.

Fellowship With One Another

Matthew 18:20, "For wherever two or three people have come together in my name, I am there, right among them."

Once we are born again, we belong to the body of Christ, and we need continual fellowship with one another in order to grow. You should pray with other believer's because we are a family and it lets you know you are not alone.

Hebrews 10:24-25, "And let us consider how to spur one another to love and to good works. Let us not forsake the assembling of ourselves together, as in the manner of some, but let us exhort one another, especially as you see the Day approaching."

Psalm 133:1-3, " Behold, how good and how pleasant it is for brothers to dwell together in unity! It is like precious oil upon the head, that runs down on the beard even Aaron's beard- and going down to the collar of his garments; as the dew of Hermon, that descends upon the mountains of Zion, for there the Lord has commanded the blessing, even life forever."

It is important that once we are born again, that we come together and fellowship with other Christians, in order that we can grow spiritually. We want to align ourselves with people who are living righteously, and living a life exemplifying Christ. We don't want to be unequally yoked with people who will pull us back into worldly things; but have a connection with people who desire to live according to the Word.

2 Corinthians 6:14-18, " Do not be unequally yoked together with unbelievers. For what fellowship has righteousness with unrighteousness? What communion has light with darkness? What agreement has Messiah with Belial? Or what part has he who believes with an unbeliever? What agreement has the temple of God with idols? For you are the temple of the living God. As God has said:

> *"I will live in them*
> *and walk with them.*
> *I will be their God,*
> *and they shall be my people.*
> *Therefore,*
> *"come out from among them*
> *and be separate,*
> *says the Lord.*
> *Do not touch what is unclean,*
> *and I will receive you."*
> *I will be a Father to you,*
> *and you shall be My sons and daughters,*
> *says the Lord Almighty."*

"We must cherish **one another**, watch over **one another**, comfort **one another**, and gain instruction that we may all sit down in heaven together." "**Fellowship** is a place of grace, where mistakes aren't rubbed in but rubbed out. **Fellowship** happens when mercy wins over justice."

"Fellowship is a mutual bond that Christians have with Christ that puts us in a deep, eternal relationship with one another."

Psalm 55:14

"We took pleasant counsel together, and walked to the house of God in company."

Acts 2:42

"They continued steadfastly in the Apostles teaching and fellowship, in the breaking of bread and in the prayers."

1 John 1:7

"But if we walk in the Light as He Himself is in the Light, we have fellowship with one another, and the blood of Jesus His Son cleanses us from all sin."

1 John 1:3

"What we have seen and heard we proclaim to you also, so that you too may have fellowship with us; and indeed our fellowship is with the Father, and with His Son Jesus Christ."

Hebrews 13:16

"And do not neglect doing good and sharing, for with such sacrifices God is pleased."

Psalm 34:3

"Oh, magnify the Lord with me, and let us exalt His name."

1 Samuel 20:42,

"Jonathan said to David, "Go in peace, since the two of us swore in the name of the Lord, saying, 'The Lord will be between me and you, and between my descendants and your descendants forever." So he arose and departed, but Jonathan went into the city."

Scripture Matching

Draw a line matching the verse with scripture.

2 Corinthians 13:14	"They devoted themselves to the Apostles teaching and to fellowship, to the breaking of bread and to prayer."
Acts 2:42	"We proclaim to you what we have seen and heard, so that you also may have fellowship with us. And our fellowship is with the Father and with His son, Jesus Christ."
1 Corinthians 1:9	"But if we walk in the light, as he is in the light, we have fellowship with one another, and the blood of Jesus his son, purifies us from all sin."
1 John 1:7	"A day the grace of the Lord Jesus Christ, and the love of God, and the fellowship of the Holy Spirit be with you all."
1 John 1:3	"God is faithful, and by Him you were called to the fellowship of His Son, Yeshua the Messiah our Lord."

Proverbs 27:17, "Iron sharpens iron; so a man sharpeneth the countenance of his friend."

If you cultivate the habit of fellowshipping with the brethren, the possibility of your backsliding diminishes. This provides opportunities for encouraging each other in the Lord. When you are in the midst of Christian brothers and sisters who are constantly exhorting you, you will most likely be able to stand firm against the wiles of Satan.

Christian Fellowship

1 John 4:7	"Love one another"
Hebrews 10:25	"Encouraging one another"
Ephesians 5	"Ministering to one another"
Ephesians 6	"Pray for one another"
Galatians 5:13	"Serve one another"
1 Thessalonians 5:15	"Retaliate against one another"
Ephesians 4:32	"Forgiving one another"
Romans 16:16	"Greet one another with a holy kiss"
Psalm 16:3	"Glorifying God together"
1 Samuel 20:42	"Friendship centered in the Lord"
1 Samuel 18:1-4	"Becoming one in spirit"
1 Samuel 11:15	"Fellowship offerings"
Leviticus 26:1-13	"Divine promise of fellowship"

When You Commit to and Embrace Fellowship with God's People

1. You become aware of God-given opportunities to grow in kindness and forgiving others. (Ephesians 4:32).

2. You receive God-given opportunities to develop patience. (Ephesians 4:1-2).

3. You use your new found freedom for the loving service of others. (Gal. 5:13).

4. You gain opportunities for joy, mutual comfort, unity, encouragement and peace. (2 Cor. 13:11).

5. You demonstrate a sincere love for Jesus. (1 John 4:19-20).

6. You receive the encouragement of harmony. (Rom. 15:5).

7. You experience mutual acceptance among radically different people. (Rom.15:7).

8. You demonstrate reverence to Christ. (Eph. 5:21).

Notes

Notes

Notes

CHAPTER EIGHT.

Renewing the Mind

·—·Romans 12:2,

"And not be conformed to this world: but be ye transformed by the renewing of your mind, that ye may prove what is good, and acceptable, and perfect, will of God."

Because we have lived all our lives according to the standard of this world in time past, it is necessary to renew our mind by the Word of God, to enable us to function in our Christian walk effectively.

> *There Is Nothing As Powerful As A Changed Mind!*

Proverbs 23:7, "As a man thinketh in his heart so is he." So you are in your heart how you think, and if your heart is out of whack, your life will be out of whack; because everything about your life is going to come from your heart. Your heart is going to be based on how you think. It is the same why naturally, words determine the way you think, the way you think determines the way you feel.

If you feel depressed you have to back up and find out what you are thinking about. Thoughts of heaviness and depression determines how you feel. How a man thinks in his soul and in his mind, determines how his life will work out. So the renewing of your mind will help you transform your life. (mind management).

1. Question: Do you want to transform your life?

2. Question: Do you want to change your life to a better quality of life?

Proverbs 2:6 "For the Lord gives wisdom from his mouth come knowledge and understanding."

3 John 2 "Beloved , I wish above all things that thou mayest prosper and be in health, even as thy soul prospereth."

The mind is the battleground. The fight is in our minds. The question everyday of your life needs to be what are you thinking about? And how long are you thinking about it? How long you think about a thing is called focus. Whatever you focus on you give strength to. If you focus on your weaknesses, sins, past failures, you strengthen those things to hinder you in your present day and in your future.

Your personality is the expression of your mind. Your perception has everything to do with your progression. If you do not perceive your situation correctly, it will not be better; hence the awakening deals with your perception.

Prayer

Father, I pray that the eyes of our understanding be enlightened, that we might know that we can stand on the hope of your calling and know who we are, and not who we were. I know what you have in mind for our life. I know that we will not die today. We are called according to His purpose. Lord give us the mind of Christ that we will walk in the plans and purposes that you have destined for us. Guard our hearts and mind and let us not lean on our own understanding. Jesus, by your Holy Spirit, keep our minds firmly set where you want it to be focused. Transform us into the likeness and image of God! Amen.

Proverbs 4:23, mentions the importance of renewing the mind, "Above all else, guard your heart, for everything you do flows from it.."

If you find yourself struggling with toxic thoughts then meditate and affirm the Bible verses below on a regular basis to cleanse your mind.

1. "The weapons we fight with are not the weapons of the world. On the contrary, they have divine power to demolish strongholds." – 2 Corinthians 10:4

2. "Religion that God our Father accepts as pure and faultless is this: to look after orphans and widows in their distress and to keep oneself from being polluted by the world." – James 1:27

3. "Submit yourselves, then, to God. Resist the devil, and he will flee from you." – James 4:7

4. "Do not conform to the pattern of this world, but be transformed by the renewing of your mind. Then you will be able to test and approve what God's will is–his good, pleasing and perfect will." – Romans 12:2

5. "These are the people who divide you, who follow mere natural instincts and do not have the Spirit. But you, dear friends, by building yourselves up in your most holy faith and praying in the Holy Spirit, keep yourselves in God's love as you wait for the mercy of our Lord Jesus Christ to bring you to eternal life." – Jude 1:19-21

6. "Let the message of Christ dwell among you richly as you teach and admonish one another with all wisdom through psalms, hymns, and songs from the Spirit, singing to God with gratitude in your hearts." – Colossians 3:16

7. "Then you will know the truth, and the truth will set you free." – John 8:32

8. "Therefore, if anyone is in Christ, the new creation has come: The old has gone, the new is here!" – 2 Corinthians 5:17

9. "Set your minds on things above, not on earthly things." – Colossians 3:2

10. "The mind governed by the flesh is death, but the mind governed by the Spirit is life and peace." – Romans 8:6

11. "Above all else, guard your heart, for everything you do flows from it." – Proverbs 4:23

12. "Stand firm then, with the belt of truth buckled around your waist, with the breastplate of righteousness in place, and with your feet fitted with the readiness that comes from the gospel of peace. In addition to all this, take up the shield of faith, with which you can extinguish all the flaming arrows of the evil one." – Ephesians 6:14-16

13. "If any of you lacks wisdom, you should ask God, who gives generously to all without finding fault, and it will be given to you. But when you ask, you must believe and not doubt, because the one who doubts is like a wave of the sea, blown and tossed by the wind. That person should not expect to receive anything from the Lord." – James 1:5-7

14. "Finally, brothers and sisters, whatever is true, whatever is noble, whatever is right, whatever is pure, whatever is lovely, whatever is admirable–if anything is excellent or praiseworthy–think about such things." – Philippians 4:8

15. "Therefore, since we are surrounded by such a great cloud of witnesses, let us throw off everything that hinders and the sin that so easily entangles. And let us run with perseverance the race marked out for us," – Hebrews 12:1

16. "Do not be anxious about anything, but in every situation, by prayer and petition, with thanksgiving, present your requests to God. And the peace of God, which transcends all understanding, will guard your hearts and your minds in Christ Jesus." – Philippians 4:6-7

17. "Create in me a clean heart, O God, And renew a steadfast spirit within me." – Psalm 51:10

18. "Yet those who wait for the LORD Will gain new strength; They will mount up with wings like eagles, They will run and not get tired, They will walk and not become weary." – Isaiah 40:31

19. "Therefore we do not lose heart, but though our outer man is decaying, yet our inner man is being renewed day by day." – 2 Corinthians 4:16

Five Steps to Renewing Your Mind

Step 1: Ask the Lord to guard and direct your mind.

Step 2: Recognize the source of self-focused and self-defeating thoughts.

Step 3: Replace self-focused thinking with a God-focused mindset.

Step 4: Rest in the truth that you are accepted in Jesus Christ.

Step 5: Repeat steps 1-4 daily.

How Do You Keep Your Mind From Dwelling On Unhealthy?

Notes

Notes

Notes

CHAPTER NINE

Witnessing

Romans 1:16, "For I am not ashamed of the gospel of Christ: for it is the power of God unto salvation to everyone that believeth; to the Jew first, and also to the Greek."

There are two kinds of Christian witnessing. The first is by the way you live your life, and the second is by verbally telling someone what Jesus has and wants to do for them. Witnessing is sharing the good news about Jesus Christ, how he died for our sins, and sharing with them the opportunity to get to know him.

Matthew 28:19-20, "Go therefore and make disciples of all nations, baptizing them in the name of the Father and the Son and of the Holy Spirit, teaching them to observe all that I have commanded you; and lo, I am with you always, to the close of the age."

How Can You Be A Witness For Jesus?

Effective Soul Winning

Mark 16:15-18, "He said to them, "Go into all the world and preach the gospel to all creation. Whoever believes and is baptized will be saved, but whoever does not believe will be condemned. And these signs will accompany those who believe: In my name they will drive out demons, they will speak in new tongues; they will pick up snakes with their hands; and when they drink deadly poison, it will not hurt them at all; they will place their hands on sick people, and they will get well."

1. The Soul-Winner Must Be Compassionate (Matthew 9:36)

    a. Every sinner is spiritually lost (Luke 19:10).

    b. Every believer must be concerned about the eternal destiny of unbelievers.

    c. Every believer should be sensitive by the ravages caused by sin (John 11:35).

2. The Soul-Winner Must Be Prepared (Ephesians 6:15)

    a. Tenacity of purpose (Acts 20:22-24)

    b. A confident assurance of one's salvation (1 John 5:13, John 5:24)

    c. A working knowledge of the Word (II Tim. 2:15)

    d. A tactful approach (II Tim. 2:15)

    e. Power from on high (Luke 24:49; Acts 1:8)

    f. Praying for oneself and for souls (1 Tim. 2:1; James 1:6-7)

3. The Approach

    a. Show the prospect that all have sinned (Romans 3:23; 6:23)

    b. Show the prospect that Christ died for their sins (Romans 5:8)

    c. Show the prospect how to accept Christ as Savior (Romans 10:8-10)

    d. Resolve any difficulties that may hinder them from taking the step

4. What's The Next Step?

    a. Encourage the new believer to receive the baptism of the Holy Spirit

    b. Encourage the person to confess Christ to others at the earliest opportunity

    c. Encourage the person to read the Bible everyday (1 Peter 2:2)

    d. Encourage the person to pray every day (1 Thess. 5:17)

    e. Encourage the person to become a loyal member of a spirit-filled church (Heb. 10:25)

"Talk to someone about Christ today, lie who win a soul over to Him is wise"

What does the Bible say?

1. Matthew 4:19, Jesus called out to them, "Come, follow me, and I will show you how to fish for people!"

2. Isaiah 55:11, "so is my word that goes out from my mouth: It will not return to me empty, but will accomplish what I desire and achieve the purpose for which I sent it."

3. Matthew 24:14, "And this gospel of the kingdom will be proclaimed throughout the whole world as a testimony to all nations, and then the end will come."

4. 1 Peter 3:15, "Instead, you must worship Christ as Lord of your life. And if someone asks about your Christian hope, always be ready to explain it."

5. Mark 16:15-16, "And he said unto them, Go ye into all the world, and preach the gospel to every creature. He that believeth and is baptized shall be saved; but he that believeth not shall be damned."

6. Romans 10:15, "And how can anyone preach unless they are sent? As it is written: "How beautiful are the feet of those who bring good news!"

7. Matthew 9:37-38, "Then he said to his disciples, "The harvest is plentiful but the workers are few. Ask the Lord of the harvest, therefore, to send out workers into his harvest field."

8. Matthew 5:16, "In the same way, let your light shine before others, that they may see your good deeds and glorify your Father in heaven."

Do not be ashamed

9. Romans 1:16, "For I am not ashamed of this Good News about Christ. It is the power of God at work, saving everyone who believes–the Jew first and also the Gentile."

10. 2 Timothy 1:8, "So do not be ashamed of the testimony about our Lord or of me his prisoner. Rather, join with me in suffering for the gospel, by the power of God."

The Holy Spirit will help

11. Luke 12:12, "For the Holy Ghost shall teach you in the same hour what ye ought to say."

12. Matthew 10:20, "For it will not be you speaking, but the Spirit of your Father speaking through you."

13. Romans 8:26, "Likewise the Spirit helps us in our weakness. For we do not know what to pray for as we ought, but the Spirit himself intercedes for us with groanings too deep for words."

14. 2 Timothy 1:7, "For God gave us a spirit not of fear, but of power, and love, and self-control."

Preach the Gospel

15. 1 Corinthians 15:1-4, "Now, brothers and sisters, I want to remind you of the gospel I preached to you, which you received and on which you have taken your stand. By this gospel you are saved, if you hold firmly to the word I preached to you. Otherwise, you have believed in vain. For what I received I

passed on to you as of first importance that Christ died for our sins according to the Scriptures, that he was buried, that he was raised on the third day according to the Scriptures."

16. Romans 3:23-28, "For all have sinned and fall short of the glory of God, and all are justified freely by his grace through the redemption that came by Christ Jesus. God presented Christ as a sacrifice of atonement, through the shedding of his blood to be received by faith. He did this to demonstrate his righteousness, because in his forbearance he had left the sins committed beforehand unpunished. He did it to demonstrate his righteousness at the present time, so as to be just and the one who justifies those who have faith in Jesus. Where, then, is boasting? It is excluded. Because of what law? The law that requires works? No, because of the law that requires faith. For we maintain that a person is justified by faith apart from the works of the law."

17. John 3:3, "Jesus answered and said unto him, Verily, verily, I say unto thee, except a man be born again, he cannot see the kingdom of God."

Reminders

18. 2 Timothy 3:16, "All Scripture is God-breathed and is useful for teaching, rebuking, correcting and training in righteousness."

19. Ephesians 4:15, "Rather, speaking the truth in love, we are to grow up in every way into him who is the head, into Christ."

20. 2 Peter 3:9, "The Lord is not slow in keeping his promise, as some understand slowness. Instead he is patient with you, not wanting anyone to perish, but everyone to come to repentance."

21. Ephesians 5:15-17, "Be very careful, then, how you live—not as unwise but as wise, making the most of every opportunity, because the days are evil. Therefore do not be foolish, but understand what the Lord's will is."

Bible examples

22. Acts 1:8, "But you will receive power when the Holy Spirit has come upon you; and you shall be My witnesses both in Jerusalem, and in all Judea and Samaria, and even to the remotest part of the earth."

23. Mark 16:20, "And the disciples went everywhere and preached, and the Lord worked through them, confirming what they said by many miraculous signs."

24. Jeremiah 1:7-9, "But the Lord said to me, "Do not say, 'I am too young.' You must go to everyone I send you to and say whatever I command you. Do not be afraid of them, for I am with you and will rescue you," declares the Lord. Then the Lord reached out his hand and touched my mouth and said to me, "I have put my words in your mouth."

25. Acts 5:42, "And daily in the temple, and in every house, they ceased not to teach and preach Jesus Christ."

Notes

Notes

Notes

CHAPTER TEN.

Christian Leadership

Becoming A Leader

Leadership is the ability to inspire and influence a group of people to achieve worthwhile goals. The greatest need of humility is leadership, because everything rises and falls on leadership. The Great Commission is a leadership mandate. Jesus Christ, the greatest leader of all times expects every Christian to become a leader, (Matthew 28:18-20, Isa. 9:6, Matt 5:13-16).

1. **The Making Of A Leader**

    a. Leaders are ordinary people who release their potentials in the attempt to overcome extraordinary challenges (1 Sam. 17:20-58; II Cor. 1:3/4).

    b. The quickest route to leadership is problem solving. Luke 4:18

    c. God changes a leader before He uses the leader to create change.

2. **Cost To Leadership**

    a. Self- discipline is a non-negotiable price (1 Cor. 9:24-27; 1 Cor 6:12).

    b. Live your life on a crusade (Mark 9:34/35, John 12:24).

3. **The Characteristics And Qualities Of A Leader**

    a. Leaders initiate change (Matt. 5:43-45)- Moses. People don't like change but it is inevitable.

    b. Leaders have a sense of divine timing (1Chron. 12:32, Eccl 3:1). Timing is everything.

    c. Leaders know and focus on what is important (Acts 6:2-4; Phil. 3:13).

    d. Leaders see the invisible (Prov. 29:16; 27:12).

    e. Leaders are totally committed (Acts 20:24). Proof is action.

    f. Leaders connect with people (Acts 20:36-38).

    g. Leaders believe in possibilities (Phil. 4:13). Develop positive attitudes.

    h. Leaders are winners (1 Sam. 18:6,7). Raise the standards.

    i. Leaders are learners (Prov. 1:5) Leaders are Readers. Keep improving daily.

    j. Leaders have integrity (Acts 20:33). Transparent in their dealings.

    k. Leaders are spirit-filled (Acts 6:13; 1 Sam. 16:13).

4. **The Essence Of Leadership**

The essence of leadership is service (Mark 10:42-45).

True leaders love people more than position. True leaders grow people. They are not here because of you. You are here because of them. Don't use them to achieve your dreams. Help them to achieve theirs, and they will in turn, help you achieve yours.

Understanding Leadership

Leadership is the ability to influence a group of people towards the achievements of worthy goals. Everything rises and falls on leadership. So God is always on the search for men and women that He can work with (Jer. 5:1). Aspiring to leadership in order to serve God and the Church is an honorable ambition (1 Tim. 3:1; Jer. 45:5).

1. **PURPOSE OF LEADERSHIP**

    a. The purpose of leadership is not to produce followers (Heb. 5:12).

    b. The purpose of leadership is to produce leaders (John 20:21).

2. **QUALIFICATIONS FOR LEADERSHIP (1 Tim. 3:1-7)**

    a. Social

    b. Ethical

    c. Temperament

    d. Maturity

    e. Intellectual

    f. Domestic

3. **QUALITIES ESSENTIAL FOR LEADERSHIP**

    a. Discipline (1.Cor. 9:25)

    b. Vision (Proverbs 29:18)

    c. Wisdom (Acts 6:3)

    d. Decision (Josh 24:15)

    e. Courage (Josh 1:6-7)

f. Humility (Jam 4:6)

g. Humor (Prov. 15:13)

h. Indignation (Jn 2:13-16)

i. Patience and endurance (Jam. 1:2-4)

j. Fellowship and Friendship (Prov. 8:24)

k. Inspirational Power (2 Chron 35:2)

l. Tact and Diplomacy (Prov. 15:1)

4. RESPONSIBILITIES OF LEADERSHIP

a. To serve (Matt. 20:28)

b. To discipline (Gal. 6:1)

c. To guide (John 10:4)

d. To initiate (1 Sam 14:6-7)

e. To undertake responsibility (Jer. 1:6-7)

"Leadership by product, your results will determine your level of respect"

MEMORY VERSE: II TIMOTHY 2:2

Leaders Communicate Vision to Empower and Direct

In the book of Acts, Jesus speaks His final words to His men before ascending to heaven. Even though they are now leaders, not merely followers, they ask Jesus when His kingdom would come (Acts 1:6). Jesus doesn't tell them, but instead communicates a vision about reaching the world (1:8). His men thought *defense*; Jesus wanted them to think *offense*.

Jesus instructed them to stay in Jerusalem until they received the power they needed, then they were to go out, expanding little by little. They were to start with Jerusalem, then move to the rest of Judea, then expand to Samaria, and ultimately to the ends of the earth. This was no man-made vision, but a God-given vision.

Man-Made Vision

1. Created based on human gifts and skills
2. Fulfilled by staying ahead of others

3. Sees similar organizations as competitors

4. Aims to grow the organization and generate revenue

5. Stress may emerge both inwardly and outwardly

6. May be dropped for something better

God-Given Vision

1. Received as a revelation

2. Fulfilled through obedience

3. Sees similar organizations as complementary

4. Aims to serve people and advance God's rule

5. Accompanied by inward peace and outward opposition

6. Compelling and captivating until fulfilled

Draw A Line To Match The Leadership Qualities With Each Leader

1. Noah	a. Leaders maintain their resolve without regard for consequences
2. Abraham	b. Leaders rise to the occasion
3. Joseph	c. Leaders are not afraid of giants
4. Moses	d. Leaders embrace the unknown
5. Joshua	e. Leaders stick up for their people
6. David	f. Leaders endure in-spite of circumstances
7. Isaiah	g. Leaders are servants

8. Daniel	h. Leaders recover from failure
9. John the Baptist	I. Leaders aren't afraid to call out the phonies
10. Jesus	J. Leaders are passionate for what they believe in
11. Peter	k. Leaders do what's right even if they are alone
12. Paul	L. Leaders rule by example rather than command

Notes

Notes

Notes

CHAPTER ELEVEN.

Live For Jesus

Philippians 2:10, "that at the name of Jesus every knee should bow, of those in heaven, and of those on earth, and of those under the earth, and that every tongue should confess that Jesus Christ is Lord, to the glory of God the Father."

As Christians, our lives and our love should model the teachings that Jesus exhibited. Our lives should be radically different. We are not in charge of our lives, Jesus is. Jesus gave his life for us, so that we have life abundantly.

Jesus is our "model" for living. Our actions should be reflected in how we live daily; how we speak, think, and how we carry ourselves. Our lives should be radically different. John 17:16, "They are not of the world, just as I am not of the world."

How Can Christians Be In The World, But Not of The World?

1. NT. Cosmos- inhabited earth. People who live on Earth, Satan is the ruler of the cosmos.

    ❖ We are no longer ruled by Satan.

    ❖ We are not bound by the principles of the World.

- ❖ We are no longer ruled by sin.

- ❖ We are being changed into the image of Christ, causing our interest in the things of the world to become less and less as we mature in Christ.

2. Believer's in Jesus Christ simply are simply in the world; physically present, but not of it.

    a. Not part of its values (John 17:14-15).

    b. We should be set apart from the world.

    c. Living holy and being holy.

    d. Not to engage in sinful activities the world promotes.

    e. Not to retain the insipid, corrupt mind that the world creates.

    f. We are to conform ourselves, our minds to that of Jesus. This is a daily activity and commitment.

We are to be a light to those who are in spiritual darkness. When people see you, they should say, there something different about you. They should know us by our fruits. (Galatians 5:22).

When we live in the world, we can enjoy the things of this world; such as Gods beautiful creation He has given us. We are not to immerse ourselves in what the world values, nor are we to chase after worldly pleasures. Our thinking should model the Bible and everything Jesus taught us.

How Well do You Know Jesus

1 Peter 2:21, " For _____ have been called for this purpose, since Christ also suffered for you, leaving you an example for you to follow in _____ steps."

Philippians 2:3-8, " Do nothing from_____ or _____ , but with _____of mind regard one another as more important than yourselves; do not merely look out for your own personal interests, but also for the interests of others. Have this attitude in yourselves which has also in _____, who although He existed in the form of God, did not regard equality with God a thing to be grasped, but emptied Himself, taking the form of a bond-servant, and being made in the likeness of men. Being found in appearance as a man, He_____ Himself by becoming obedient to the point of death, even death on a cross."

2 Corinthians 3:18, "But we all, with unveiled face, beholding as in a mirror the glory of the Lord, are being _____ into the same image from _____ to _____, just as from the Lord, the Spirit."

John 13:34, "A new_____ I give to you, that you love one another, even as I have loved you, that you also love one another."

1 Corinthians 11:1, "Be _____of me, just as I also am of Christ."

1 John 2:6, "The one who says he abides in Him ought himself to _____ in the same manner as He walked."

Ephesians 4:32, " Be kind to one another, tender-hearted, _____each other, just as God in Christ also has _____ you."

10 Steps To Grow In Christ

1. **Pray** - 1 Thessalonians says, "We are to pray without ceasing." When we pray, we are able to overcome life's challenges. Our faith will increase and we will grow strong in the Lord. Prayer is our personal, intimate time with God. It is how we communicate with one another. Our Heavenly Father desires a close relationship with us. Our model for prayer is in Matthew 6:9-13.

2. **Live As God Called Us** We are sons and daughters of the most High King. We are precious in His eyes. We are to live a life that is a reflection of Christ Jesus. We are to live a life that is full of God's love, cultivate good habits, helping others, and worshipping God.

3. **Follow Christ Teachings.** Following Jesus means to apply his teachings in our everyday lives. "If you hold to my teachings, you are really my disciples. Then you will know the truth, and the truth will set you free." (John 8:31-32).

4. **Honor God**- 1 Corinthians 10:31, teaches believers to honor the Lord in all we do, "whether therefore ye eat, or drink, or whatsoever ye do, do all to the glory of God." Here are seven ways to honor God with our bodies and keep ourselves healthy.

    a) Moving your body…

    b) Drinking enough water…

    c) Eating nutritious foods…

    d) Seeking proper medical care and following through…

    e) Taking action to reduce stress.

    f) Avoiding things that are damaging to our bodies.

5. **Love Your Neighbors-** Mark 12:30-31, "You shall love the Lord your God with all your heart, and with all your soul, and with all your mind, and with all your strength. This is the first commandment. The second is this, You shall love your neighbor as yourself. There is no other commandment greater than these."

6. **Stick To Good And To Righteousness-** 2 Corinthians 6:14-18, "Do not be unequally yoked with unbelievers, For what partnership has righteousness with lawlessness? Or what fellowship has light with darkness? What accord has Christ with Belial? Or what portion does a believer share with an unbeliever? What agreement has the temple of the living God; as God said, "I will make my dwelling among them and walk among them, and I will be their God, and they shall be my people. Therefore go out of the midst, and be separate from them, says the Lord, and touch no unclean thing; then I will welcome you, and I will be a father to you, and you shall be sons and daughters to me, says the Lord Almighty."

7. **Read The Bible-** 2 Timothy, 2:15, "Study to show thyself approved unto God, a workman that needeth not to be ashamed, rightly dividing the word of truth." The Bible shows us God's character and provides us His revelation of himself to His people. Reading the Bible regularly reorients our thinking so that we can grow in maturity, which is part of the Christian calling (Ephesians 4:14-16; Romans 12:1-2).

8. **Share Your Gifts-** We all have special gifts inside of us. Some of us are living in it and making a living from it. These gifts are unique to you. The gifts that each of us possess are meant to be shared with the world. Here are some reasons why:

- ❖ To inspire others
- ❖ Make new connections
- ❖ Cheer someone up
- ❖ Self-confidence soars
- ❖ Income source

9. **Encourage Our Fellow Man-** Proverbs 27:17, " Iron sharpens iron, so a man sharpens the countenance of his friend." God expects us to live and serve in a community of other believers, and He desires for us to build loving and growing relationships with others. 'Iron sharpening iron' requires a level of accountability or a personal inclination; to allow significant others to look close enough in our lives, so that they can see the specific weaknesses or problem areas. Genuine accountability demands that the person receiving the counsel or advice, is willing to allow the friend (s) to look for the vulnerabilities in their lives. To accept what they point out, and then do something to fix it when they hear it.

10. **Co-operate With Others-** Amos 3:3, "Do two people walk together, if they have not agreed?"

Philippians 2:1-30, "So if there is any encouragement in Christ, any comfort from love, any participation in the Spirit, any affection and sympathy, complete my joy by being of the same mind, having the same love, being in full accord and one mind. Do nothing from rivalry or conceit, but in humility count others more significant than yourselves. Let each of you look not only to his own interests, but also to the interests of others. Have this mind among yourselves, which is yours in Christ Jesus."

Notes

Notes

Notes

Bibliography

Anderson, K. *Where to find it in the bible* (printed.).

(1996). Thomas Nelson.

www.shutterstock.com

The Supernatural Bible by Passio (2017).

Appendix

Chapter 1, Page 4

1. Pondering, Preaching, and Applying

2. Remembering, Truths, Praises, and Promises

5. Remember, Ponder, and Meditate

6. Truth and Draws

8. Meditate

9. Thoughts

10. Evoking, Embracing, and Embedding

Chapter 4, Pages 34

1. F
2. T
3. T
4. T
5. T
6. T
7. T
8. F
9. T
10. T

Chapter 5, Page 44

1. T
2. T
3. T
4. F
5. T
6. T
7. T
8. F
9. T
10. F
11. F
12. T
13. T
14. T
15. T

Chapter 6, Pages 55&56

1. T
2. T
3. T
4. F
5. T
6. T
7. T
8. F
9. T
10. F
11. F
12. T
13. T

Chapter 7, Page 74

2 Cor. 13:14, "A day the grace of the Lord Jesus Christ, and the love of God, and the fellowship of the Holy Spirit be with you all."

Acts 2:42, "They devoted themselves to the Apostles teaching and to fellowship, to the breaking of bread and to prayer."

1 Cor. 1:9, "God is faithful, and by Him you were called to the fellowship of His son Yeshua the Messiah our Lord."

1 John 1:7, "But if we walk in the light, as he is in the light, we have fellowship with one another, and the blood of Jesus his son, purifies us from all sin."

1 John 1:3, "We proclaim to you what we have seen and heard, so that you also may have fellowship with us, and our fellowship is the Father and with His son, Jesus Christ."

Chapter 10, Page 101

1. K
2. D
3. F
4. E
5. L
6. C
7. B
8. A
9. I
10. G
11. H
12. J

Chapter 11, Pages 106-107

1. To this you	2. transformed
His	glory
Strife	glory
Conceit	new commandment
Humility	ye followers
Christ Jesus	walk
Humbled	forgiving
	forgave

About the Author

Michelle L. Fortune was born and raised in Youngstown, Ohio. She graduated from Youngstown State University with a Bachelor's Degree in Nursing, and Capital University with her Masters in Nursing Administration.

Michelle is currently studying at Kingdom Covenant Leadership Institute under Dr. Pat Frances for her Doctorate in Theology. Michelle is an Instructor with Lions International Training Institute School of Theology. She has a passion for teaching and mentoring people who desire a deeper relationship with God and to grow stronger in their faith. Michelle is the founder of Garments Of Praise Ministry LLC, Garments of Praise Dance Studio Subsidiary, and Virtuous Women Empowerment.

Other books by this author:

Breaking the Chains of Abuse, Silent Bondage
The Heart of a Worshiper Called to Dance
Divine Prayer Journal

Contact:

Email: kingstravel17@gmail.com
Blog: www.spiritualtruths1.blogspot.com
Website: www.michellelfortune.com

www.ingramcontent.com/pod-product-compliance
Lightning Source LLC
Chambersburg PA
CBHW081155290426
44108CB00018B/2563